**DO NOT REMOVE
CARDS FROM POCKET**

Investments and the Law

The Basic Investor's Library

Chelsea House Publishers

Investments and the Law

RACHEL S. EPSTEIN

Paul A. Samuelson
Senior Editorial Consultant

Chelsea House Publishers   New York   Philadelphia

Editor-in-Chief   Nancy Toff
Executive Editor   Remmel T. Nunn
Managing Editor   Karyn Gullen Browne
Copy Chief   Juliann Barbato
Picture Editor   Adrian G. Allen
Art Director   Giannella Garrett
Manufacturing Manager   Gerald Levine

Staff for INVESTMENTS AND THE LAW
Senior Editor   Marjorie P. K. Weiser
Associate Editor   Andrea E. Reynolds
Assistant Editor   Karen Schimmel
Copyeditor   Terrance Dolan
Deputy Copy Chief   Ellen Scordato
Editorial Assistant   Tara P. Deal
Associate Picture Editor   Juliette Dickstein
Picture Researcher   Betsy Levin
Senior Designer   Laurie Jewell
Designer   Ghila Krajzman
Production Coordinator   Joseph Romano

Consulting Editor   Shawn Patrick Burke

3   5   7   9   8   6   4

Library of Congress Cataloging in Publication Data

Epstein, Rachel S.
   Investments and the law / Rachel S. Epstein, Paul A. Samuelson.
      p. — cm.—(The Basic investor's library)
   Bibliography: p.
   Includes index.
   Summary: Discusses the legal regulations pertaining to securities
in the United States and the organizations which administer such
laws.
   ISBN 1-55546-632-X
         0-7910-0316-7 (pbk.)
   1. Investments—Law and legislation—United States—Juvenile
literature. 2. Securities—United States—Juvenile literature.
[1. Investments—Law and legislation. 2. Securities.]
I. Samuelson, Paul Anthony, 1915– —. II. Title. III. Series.
KF1070.Z9E67 1988
346.73'092—dc19
[347.30692]

                                                87-34119
                                                CIP

CONTENTS

Learning the Tools of Investing

PAUL A. SAMUELSON

When asked why the great financial house of Morgan had been so successful, J. Pierpont Morgan replied, "Do you suppose that's because we take money seriously?"

Managing our personal finances is a serious business, and something we all must learn to do. We begin life dependent on someone else's income and capital. But after we become independent, it is a remorseless fact of nature that we must not only support ourselves for the present but must also start saving money for retirement. The best theory of saving that economists have is built upon this model of *life-cycle saving:* You must provide in the long years of prime working life for what modern medicine has lengthened to, potentially, decades of retirement. This life-cycle model won a 1985 Nobel Prize for my MIT colleague Franco Modigliani, and it points up the need to learn the rudiments of personal finance.

Learning to acquire wealth, however, is only part of the story. We must also learn to avoid losing what we have acquired. There is an old saying that "life insurance is *sold*, not bought." The same goes for stocks and bonds. In each case, the broker is guaranteed a profit, whether or not the customer benefits from the transaction. Knowledge is the customer's only true ally in the world of finance. Some gullible victims have lost their lifetime savings to unscrupulous sales promoters. One chap buys the Brooklyn Bridge. Another believes a stranger who asserts that gold will quickly double in price, with no risk of a drop in value. Such "con" (confidence) rackets get written up in the newspapers and on the police blotters every day.

I am concerned, however, about something less dramatic than con artists; something that is not at all illegal, but that costs ordinary citizens a thousand times more than outright embezzlement or fraud. Consider two families, neighbors who could be found in any town. They started alike. Each worked equally hard, and had about the same income. But the Smiths have to make do with half of what the Joneses have in retirement income, for one simple reason: The Joneses followed prudent practice as savers and investors, while the Smiths tried to make a killing and constantly bought and sold stocks at high commissions.

The point is, it does matter to learn how financial markets work, and how you can participate in them to your best advantage. It is important to know the difference between *common* and *preferred* stocks, between *convertible* and *zero-coupon* bonds. It is not difficult to find out what *mutual funds* are, and to understand the difference between the successful Fund A, which charges no commission, or "load," and the equally successful Fund B, which does charge the buyer such a fee.

All investing involves risk. When I was a young assistant professor, I said primly to my great Harvard teacher, Joseph Schumpeter: "We should speculate only with money we can afford to lose." He gently corrected me: "Paul, there is no such money. Besides, a speculator is merely an investor who has lost." Did Schumpeter exaggerate? Of course he did, but in the good cause of establishing the basic point of financial management: Good past performance is no guarantee of the future.

That is why *diversification* is the golden rule. "Don't put all your eggs in one basket. And watch all those baskets!" However, diversification does not mean throwing random darts at the financial pages of the newspaper to choose the best stocks in which to invest. The most diversified strategy of all would be to invest in a portfolio containing all the stocks in the comprehensive Standard & Poor's 500 Stock Index. But rather than throw random darts at the financial pages to pick out a few stocks, why not throw a large bath towel at the newspaper instead? Buy a bit of everything in proportion to its value in the larger world: Buy more General Motors than Ford, because GM is the bigger company; buy General Electric as well as GM because the auto industry is just one of many industries. That is called being an *index investor*. Index investing makes sense because 70 out of 100 investors who try to do better than the Standard & Poor's 500, the sober record shows, do worse over a 30-year period.

Do not take my word for this. The second lesson in finance is to be skeptical of what writers and other experts say, and that includes being skeptical of professors of economics. So I wish readers *Bon voyage!* on their cruise to command the fundamentals of investing. On your mainship flag, replace the motto "Nothing ventured, nothing gained" with the Latin words *Caveat emptor*—Let the buyer beware.

The New York Stock Exchange, ca. 1900.

Investments and the Law

W e recommend an act to restrain the number and ill practices of brokers . . . to stop people from buying stocks and artfully enhancing their reputation [to raise their prices], then selling the shares to ignorant men." These words, written 400 years ago by a special parliamentary commission in London, mark the beginning of the story of investments and the law. This story is still being written today, as the United States Congress considers possible new laws to regulate the securities industry.

This book looks first at some early problems in the investment and business world, and some of the regulations designed to deal with them. It then discusses the securities laws and the work of the regulatory agencies that administer them. Finally, it describes ways in which investors can protect themselves against illegal or unethical practices, and provides some information about careers in investments and the law.

REASONS FOR REGULATING THE INVESTMENT INDUSTRY

Lured by lavish promises, British citizens rushed to invest in the South Sea Company in 1720. After the company's directors unloaded their stock when the price rose, the price plummeted. The event became known as the South Sea Bubble.

O ver the years, governments have issued many laws regulating the buying and selling of securities. In the United States these laws, on a federal level, go back only to 1933. In England, as the quotation that opens this book indicates, they go back much farther. The securities law passed 400 years ago in response to the commission report was changed 150 years later when an investment abuse exploded in scandal. The British government had granted the South Sea Company the valuable right to be the exclusive trading agent for South America and the Pacific islands. The South Sea Company sold shares to the public to finance its trading activities. Each share rose in price from £128.5 in January 1720 to £1,000 in July of that year—and then plummeted to £125 in December. The directors of the company made £5 million by selling stock at the top price. When the bubble burst, thousands of people at every level of society were ruined. The disaster that came to be known as the South Sea Bubble resulted in the so-called "Bubble Act" of 1720. It prohibited inaccurate statements in corporate charters and provided penalties for brokers who sold shares of stock in inaccurately represented enterprises.

There are many laws and regulations that govern the issuing and trading of securities in the United States today. Laws are passed by Congress and are usually broad in scope, occasionally setting up agencies to deal with sets of related problems. Regulations are more specific, and are issued by the agencies designated by Congress. The role of Congress in the nation's economic life is derived from Article I, Section 8 of the Constitution, which states that "the Congress shall have Power . . . To regulate Commerce with foreign Nations, and among the several States."

A major reason for the large number of regulations affecting the investment industry is that buying and selling securities involves the possibility of enormous gains and losses. Also, unlike most other items, securities are not bought directly by the purchaser. Instead, an investor must use the services of an account executive (AE, also known as a stockbroker or registered representative) at a brokerage firm. Brokers may unscrupulously follow their own interests instead of their clients'. They may, for example, urge clients to buy and sell securities too frequently, for the sole purpose of generating commissions on every transaction (a practice known as *churning*). Brokers may recommend securities that are inappropriate for a client's needs, especially those that are risky (have a high probability of loss). Stock prices may be manipulated through trading by brokers and investors who have inside information.

The goals of the U.S. securities laws are, first, to protect investors from manipulation and other abuses in the securities markets, and second, to ensure that investors have full access to information about companies whose shares are publicly traded.

HISTORY OF REGULATION IN THE UNITED STATES

After the Civil War, the United States began to transform itself from a nation of small farmers, shop owners, and manufacturers into the greatest industrial nation in the world. On the way to achieving that status there were problems that had to

An 1875 engraving of a train being loaded with barrels of oil. As the major means of shipping, railroads often set favored rates for some customers.

This 1883 political cartoon comments on the wealth controlled by John D. Rockefeller, who in 1882 had created the Standard Oil trust.

be solved. Three problem areas were unfair charges by railroads, destruction of competition by monopolies and trusts, and the instability of banks. Eventually, Congress was called upon to solve all of these problems. These early laws paved the way for the regulation of the securities industry that is in effect today.

Unfair Pricing by Railroads   After the Civil War, railroad lines expanded rapidly, soon becoming the major means of transportation in the United States. Because rail transportation was so much in demand, many of the industry's managers were tempted to abuse their power. One of the most persistent and harmful abuses was the practice of charging higher shipping rates to small companies than to large ones for the same trip. For example, in a six-month period in 1880, the New York Central Railroad granted more than 6,000 special rates to favored customers, usually large companies.

When farmers and small-business owners demanded laws to curb the abuses of the railroads, state legislatures began to act. Hoping to avoid legislative curbs, the railroads offered lavish bribes to politicians and judges.

Finally, in 1887, Congress passed the Interstate Commerce Act, which stated the general principle that all rates must be just and reasonable, and established the Interstate Commerce Commission to carry out its provisions. The act prohibited the offering of preferential treatment among shippers for different localities and types of freight. All rates and fares were to be printed and publicly posted. As the first federal regulation of business activity, the Interstate Commerce Act paved the way for the regulations that followed.

Monopolies and Trusts   The years from 1880 to 1905 saw enormous growth in both the size and number of America's largest corporations, particularly those involving heavy industry, electric utilities, railroads, and the processing of raw materials such as petroleum, steel, tobacco, and sugar. Due to lower costs of manufacturing in large quantities, these companies could afford to sell their products at lower prices, forcing smaller firms to lower their prices, too. As the small companies lost more and more money, the large firms were able to buy them out at bargain prices. Eliminating competitors in this fashion, the remaining company became a monopoly, controlling virtually an entire industry. Alone in the field, it would then sharply raise prices, in effect extorting money from customers who now had nowhere else to go. Historian Samuel Eliot Morison has written that this "was a period of cutthroat competition in which the big fish swallowed the little fish and then tried to eat one another."

An 1888 political cartoon by Thomas Nast satirizes Secretary of State James G. Blaine, who had defended trusts on the grounds that England's free trade system was "plastered over" with trusts.

Some people figured out a way to gain control over a group of publicly held companies by combining them into a trust—a combination of firms or corporations formed by a legal agreement. Shareholders in the smaller companies received trust certificates in exchange for their stock, entitling them to a share of ownership and profits in the new, large company but not to any voting privileges. The trust came to be one giant company controlled by a board of trustees. The trustees had absolute power and often used it to control prices and eliminate competition. Again, by artificially lowering prices, a trust could drive holdout companies into bankruptcy or force them to sell out to the trust at a disadvantageous price. The trust concept was pioneered by John D. Rockefeller, who in 1882 put together the Standard Oil trust from 77 smaller companies and then ran it with 8 other trustees.

As power became concentrated in large corporations and trusts, farmers and small-business owners began to oppose them. These groups were being hurt by the high prices charged by trusts for raw materials and merchan-

Ohio senator John Sherman, author of the 1890 Sherman Anti-Trust Act, in a photograph by Mathew Brady.

dise, as well as by the high rates charged by railroads for moving their products to market.

In 1890 Congress passed the Sherman Anti-Trust Act, which stated that "every contract, combination in the form of trust or otherwise, or conspiracy, in restraint of trade or commerce among the several states or with foreign nations, is hereby declared to be illegal."

However, the Sherman Act was ineffective in putting an end to the abuses of monopolies and trusts. There were three reasons for this. First, efforts to use Sherman to halt the actions of monopolies and trusts were challenged in court by those powerful organizations. Rulings and appeals took years, and when a case finally reached the Supreme Court the law was often interpreted in a way that let an enormous company remain enormous.

Second, no administrative machinery had been set up to enforce the law. Under the Sherman Act, suits against companies had to be brought by the president of the United States, who often had no desire to oppose the business interests that had helped elect him.

Finally, when violators who were brought to trial were convicted, the fines imposed were amazingly low. Acting illegally in defiance of the Sherman Act brought in enough money to easily cover the amount of the fine and still leave a generous profit.

Around the turn of the century, many magazine articles and books appeared that described the evils of the giant corporations. These evils included exploiting the workers, especially women and children, selling impure food and drugs, and acting without regard for the country's natural resources. At the same time the Populist party became widely influential, especially in the Midwest. It advocated various measures to give farmers, workers, and small-business people more equitable treatment. Among the Populists' demands were federal control of railroads and a

Left: *Syrup being added to cans of fruit around the turn of the century, when prepared foods were often contaminated. Mechanical methods of canning were later introduced to ensure better quality products.*

Right: *A campaign cartoon presents William Jennings Bryan, candidate for president on both the Democratic and Populist tickets, in 1896. Bryan held that the government should guarantee the economic security of farmers, workers, and small business owners.*

graduated income tax (a higher tax rate for higher incomes) at a time when there was no national tax on income.

To remedy the defects of the Sherman Act, Congress passed the Clayton Act in 1914. Clayton was more specific than Sherman in defining the monopolistic practices that were prohibited. In particular, it made illegal price discrimination that had the effect of reducing competition or tended to create a monopoly. Clayton also forbade *tying contracts*, which forced buyers to take items they did not want in order to purchase those they did. In addition, it prohibited mergers that would restrict competition: It was now illegal for a company to merge with a competitor, although it was not illegal to buy stock in a competing company solely as an investment, without the intent of reducing competition. The Clayton Act also held corporate directors personally liable (responsible) for violations of law by their companies.

Also in 1914 Congress passed an act creating the Federal Trade Commission (FTC) to investigate charges of unfair and discriminatory business practices and to enforce the antitrust laws by prosecuting violators. Now some antitrust and antimonopoly laws could be enforced without having to go to court.

Banking   In the 19th century, especially after the Civil War, the economy was marked by sharp ups and downs. During periods of prosperity the railroads expanded and business owners invested in equipment for their growing

A periodical illustration depicts frantic trading on the floor of the New York Stock Exchange as prices fell sharply in the panic of 1884.

companies. To continue growing, companies needed more and more money, which they often raised through bank loans. Interest costs and demand for labor and raw materials led to higher prices for goods. When it became too costly to expand businesses, the buying and building would stop and the boom would end. As businesses contracted, borrowers became unable to pay off their loans. This led to bankruptcies to get out of debt and panic selling on the stock market to raise cash. Banks themselves often went into bankruptcy, adding to the severity of the down times; their failure meant that their business clients could not borrow the money they needed to keep going.

The panic of 1907 started with a steep fall in stock prices. Stockholders lost massive amounts of money and were unable to repay their loans from the large banks in New York—central reserve banks, which held much of the reserve money of banks around the country. The central banks had profited by making loans to stock speculators, but when the market dropped, they became unable to collect on these loans. When banks around the country began calling in their reserve funds, the central banks were unable to meet the demand. They began to fail, followed by the banks in small towns and rural areas. As the banks failed, depositors lost their money and local businesses could no longer borrow to meet operating needs. As speculators sold at whatever price they could get in order to repay their loans, stock prices dropped even further.

A crowd gathers at the corner of Ann Street and Broadway in New York City as news of the panic of 1907 spreads.

The time had come for Congress to act. The country could no longer be at the mercy of a largely private and unregulated banking system. A mechanism was needed whereby the nation's money supply could expand and contract according to the changing needs of business. The system also needed banks in which other banks could deposit their reserves and be sure of getting this money back on demand. A commission was established by Congress to study banking systems worldwide and make recommendations. These recommendations, which were reported to Congress in 1912, became the basis of the Federal Reserve Act of 1913.

The Federal Reserve Building in Washington, D.C. In 1913, Congress established the Federal Reserve System, consisting of the Federal Reserve Board in Washington and 12 district banks throughout the country.

This act established the Federal Reserve System, which consists of the Federal Reserve Board, based in Washington, D.C., and 12 district banks throughout the country. The system functions as a central bank for the government's financial transactions. It coordinates and controls commercial banking and, most important of all, supervises the nation's money supply and credit conditions by regulating the amount of money that banks are required to keep in reserve and the amount of money in circulation. All these influence interest rates.

Federal Regulation of the Securities Industry

The United States's part in World War I was financed by an enormous sale of Liberty Bonds, which represented government borrowing from the citizens of the country. Some buyers of these bonds became enthusiastic purchasers of the millions of shares of stock in new radio, automobile, and airplane companies that flooded the stock market in the 1920s. Many investors at that time were buying their stocks on *margin*—borrowing part of the purchase price from their brokers, who in turn borrowed from the banks. To stimulate the postwar economy, borrowing was made easy and interest rates kept low. At the same

The trading floor of the New York Stock Exchange after a 1918 Liberty Loan rally. The sale of Liberty bonds to citizens financed U.S. involvement in World War I.

time, commercial banks were using their depositors' money to buy stocks for investment and speculation and also to underwrite new issues of stocks. *Underwriting* is the purchase of newly issued securities from a corporation in order to sell the shares at a higher price to the investing public. The issuing company gets a large infusion of new capital to use for corporate expansion. If investors buy the stock, the underwriting broker makes a profit.

The frantic stock buying of the 1920s was often based more on hope and extravagant claims by brokers than on analysis of a company's true value or the nation's true financial health. Waves of buying pushed the stock market to spectacular new highs.

Then, on October 29, 1929, stock prices plummeted. Relatively few people—only bankers, stockholders, and brokers—were directly affected. But millions of other Americans, many of whom had never been involved with Wall Street, suffered financially because bank credit dried up. Investors who had bought stocks on margin had to borrow more money so they would not have to sell their stocks.

When investors could no longer cover their margins by borrowing, their brokers put their stock back on the market. As stock sales to cover margins increased, the market was glutted. Supply greatly exceeded demand, because few people now had cash to invest, and most feared that prices would drop even further. Indeed, that is what happened. Increasingly, borrowers—whether individuals, brokerages, businesses, or farmers—could not repay their bank loans.

Some banks failed. Frightened, people began to withdraw their money from the banks, and still more banks collapsed. There were 305 bank failures in September 1931 and 522 the following month. As the supply of money declined, businesses could no longer operate. The Great Depression had begun.

When Franklin Delano Roosevelt, who had been elected president on his promise to end the depression, was inaugurated on March 4, 1933, 15 million Americans were out of work. The banks in three states—Illinois, Michigan, and New York—had been closed on the order of their governors to prevent panic.

One of Roosevelt's first acts in office was to urge Congress to enact a law to regulate the issuing of securities. Even before Roosevelt came into office, the Senate Banking and Currency Committee had been investigating the securities industry in order to propose appropriate regulations. The committee's investigation uncovered "the complete abandonment by many underwriters and brokers of those standards of fair, honest and prudent dealing that should be basic to the encouragement of investment in any enterprise."

Among the specific problems noted by the committee were the following:

In 1930, unemployed New Yorkers stood in line at St. Peter's Mission to receive bread and coffee. Millions of Americans were affected by the 1929 stock market crash when it led to bank failures.

1. Lack of adequate information for investors about the financial condition and business activities of companies whose stock was being traded.
2. Abuse of the *proxy* (vote by mail by an investor who cannot attend a shareholders' meeting, usually entrusted to a corporate officer) by managements hoping to retain control, by the withholding of pertinent facts involving issues on which corporate charters required shareholders to vote.
3. Short-term trading by corporate insiders—usually the board of directors and top management—who took advantage of information not publicly available in order to make substantial profits.

Two laws were passed in rapid succession, the Securities Act of 1933 and the Securities Exchange Act of 1934. They had two main goals. The first was to prohibit fraud in the securities industry. The second was to require full

Supreme Court justice Louis D. Brandeis, whose social reform philosophies influenced the Securities Exchange Act of 1934.

disclosure of corporate data to assure that investment decisions could be made with accurate information about the companies whose securities were for sale. This goal was influenced by the philosophy of Louis D. Brandeis, a social reformer and lawyer who later became a justice of the Supreme Court. In 1914, in a book entitled *Other People's Money*, Brandeis had written, "Sunlight is said to be the best of disinfectants; electric light the most effective policeman." The intent of the 1933 and 1934 legislation was to shine a stong beam of light onto securities transactions.

The Securities Laws

The Securities Act of 1933, the first true consumer-protection legislation in the United States, regulates the two groups that might take advantage of the investing public: corporations that issue stocks to the public, and investment firms that actually sell those securities.

The Securities Exchange Act of 1934 established the Securities and Exchange Commission (SEC) as a government agency to administer the Securities Act of the preceding year. These two laws function together to protect the investing public.

At least 20 days before a corporation plans to offer stock to the public, it must file a registration statement with the SEC. The registration statement must fully and accurately disclose, or publicly announce, all material facts about the company and the securities it proposes to sell. The company must also file a *prospectus*—a summary form of the information contained in the registration statement—which must be given by brokers to anyone interested in buying shares after the stock is issued. Investors who suffer losses can sue and recover damages if they can prove that the registration statement contained misleading or incomplete information.

Among the information that must be disclosed are the following:

- A description of the company's businesses and properties.
- The significant provisions of the security to be offered for sale. For a bond, when it will be repaid; for a stock, whether it pays dividends; and for all securities, their relationship to previously issued securities.
- A description of the company's management.
- Financial statements, giving the company's assets, earnings, and liabilities (debts), which have been examined (audited) by independent public accountants.

The SEC examines the filed registration statements to determine whether the disclosures are accurate and in accordance with its rules. If the SEC questions anything in the registration statement or requests additional information, the company must file amendments in response. In most cases, after the last amendment is filed the registration statement becomes effective, which means the stock can then legally be sold to the public. Acceptance of a corporation's registration statement does not mean that the SEC has ruled on the value or quality of the securities being issued; it does mean that the company has fully and accurately disclosed all information that an investor might need to evaluate the security being offered for sale.

The Securities Exchange Act also required corporations whose stock is publicly traded to issue periodic disclosure reports, usually four times a year, to keep shareholders fully and accurately informed. The laws also specify that proxy solicitations—mailings to shareholders about votes to be taken—be registered with the SEC, again to be sure that all relevant information is given to shareholders.

The 1934 act also prohibited short-term trading by insiders. *Insider trading*, which was not defined by Congress, is understood to mean buying or selling stock on the basis of information that has not been made available to the public. An insider is someone who has access to such information, perhaps by being a director or manager of a company. If the information is good news for the company, an insider can make money by buying the stock and then selling it at a higher price when the good news becomes public and investors are eager to buy the stock. If the news is bad, the insider may sell before the news becomes public, when other investors would sell, thus lowering the stock's price. In both situations, the insider profits in a way that is not available to other investors.

When a company has some news about its activities that the public must know, it generally sends the information in the form of a press release to major newspapers. For example, a company that is about to sign a contract for a major sale must let the business community know about its good fortune and prospective profits. If someone who knew about the contract bought a large block of stock before the contract was publicly announced, that might be considered insider trading.

Investors can be hurt not only by the people who trade in securities but also by the companies issuing them. A company might have news that it wants to hide from the investing public, such as a change of management or the loss of a key account. The company might fear that investors would rush to sell their stocks if the news became known, thus driving stock prices down. But the Securities Exchange Act of 1934 made it illegal to withhold such information intentionally.

This law was amended in 1984 to impose stricter penalties on those who violate the insider trading prohibition. According to SEC rules, a company can recover the profit reaped by an insider on trades within six months. A few years later, though, a number of insider trading cases led to pressure on Congress to amend it further by defining an insider and listing the insider trading situations that are prohibited.

As a safeguard against insider trading, all officers, directors, and investors holding 10 percent or more of a company's stock must file an initial report with the SEC showing the extent of their ownership of the company's securities; they must then file additional reports for any month during which there is any change in their ownership position.

The 1934 act requires the Federal Reserve Board to set limits on the amount of credit that may be extended by investment firms to their clients for the purpose of buying stock by means of margin accounts. This act also directs the SEC to set rules to make the buying and selling of stocks as fair as possible.

Securities are bought and sold on stock exchanges according to an old and formalized auction-bidding system. The New York Stock Exchange (the Exchange) was founded in 1792 and has 606 member firms. It deals in the stocks of 1,632 listed companies. Member firms are the broker-dealers who can buy and sell securities on the floor of the Exchange for either themselves or their clients. These are the firms whose activities are regulated by the Exchange. The listed companies are the ones whose securities are traded on the Exchange.

The American Stock Exchange (AMEX), also located in New York City, has 576 member firms and 860 listed companies, which may be smaller than the companies listed on the New York Stock Exchange.

Stocks are also traded in the over-the-counter market (OTC) by members of the National Association of Securities Dealers (NASD). The NASD was established in accordance with a 1938 amendment to the Securities Exchange Act of 1934. OTC securities are not traded at a central exchange but are bought and sold by telephone and computer. The NASD has more than 6,600 member firms, which range from the giant investment banking firms to small "mom and pop" brokerages. The best-known activity of the NASD is the NASDAQ (National Association of Securities Dealers Automated Quotations system), which makes available to all members price quotations for all over-the-counter securities trades, through a computer network. The securities of almost 5,000 companies are cataloged by the NASDAQ system.

All major stock exchanges, brokerage firms, and individual brokers are required by the 1934 act to register with the SEC and to show that they are taking steps to protect investors. The SEC periodically investigates the exchanges and the exchanges in turn investigate their member firms to make sure that the rules are being obeyed.

Amendments to the 1934 Act   This act was amended in 1968 to protect investors in a company that is the object of a takeover attempt. One way for a company or individual to gain control of another company is by purchasing enough stock to control the voting on crucial issues. Because stock ownership is often dispersed among many investors, each of whom owns only a small fraction of the shares outstanding, it is possible to gain voting control by buying more shares than are owned by any other investor. This may be a small percentage of the shares outstanding.

The 1968 amendment, often called the Williams Act because it was sponsored by New Jersey senator Harrison Williams, requires that a person or company buying more than 10 percent of a company's outstanding shares must disclose any intent to eventually gain control of the com-

New Jersey senator Harrison Williams (left) meets with Walter Frank, a member of the New York Stock Exchange board of directors. Williams sponsored the 1968 amendment to the 1934 Securities Exchange Act requiring that takeover attempts be made public.

pany and must file the appropriate documents with the SEC.

The Williams Act also requires that this same information be made public by anyone asking shareholders to vote to accept or reject a tender offer. A *tender offer* is a request by an outside company or investor that shareholders sell (tender) their stock at a specified price. It usually represents an effort to acquire the company. This provision of the act ensures that shareholders are informed that the sale of their stock means ownership of the company may change.

In 1970, a further amendment required full disclosure by anyone seeking to acquire more than five percent of a company's outstanding stock, whether by directly negotiated purchase or by a tender offer.

Investment Company Act of 1940   This act extended to mutual funds the requirement for full disclosure through registration statements. A *mutual fund* is an investment company that sells shares and uses the resulting pooled investment to buy stocks and bonds.

Investment Advisers Act of 1940   This act regulates individuals or firms that receive fees by acting as consultants concerning the purchase or sale of securities. They must register with the SEC, keep financial and other records as the SEC specifies, and submit these records for periodic examination.

HOW THE SEC WORKS

The five commissioners of the Securities and Exchange Commission meet in the fall of 1987 at their Washington, D.C., headquarters.

The work of the SEC is carried out by five commissioners, four major divisions, and several offices that each have a specific role in enforcing the securities laws. The work is done at the commission headquarters in Washington, D.C., as well as at the nine regional and five branch (smaller offices within the regions) offices throughout the country.

The commissioners are responsible for carrying out the mission of the SEC, which is to protect the investing public. The five commissioners are appointed to five-year terms by the president, one every year on a staggered schedule, with the advice and consent of the Senate. The president selects one member, generally from his own political party, to serve as chairman. No more than three of the five commissioners may belong to the same political party, to ensure that the SEC is a non-partisan agency. The SEC is answerable to Congress. The commissioners meet to discuss and resolve issues brought to them by the staff. The issues might involve interpreting securities laws; changing or making new rules to enforce the laws in terms of current problems in the securities industry; or recommending new laws for Congress to enact. For example, in the fall of 1987 the commission submitted to Congress a proposal for a bill defining illegal use of insider information in securities trading.

The Divisions

The Division of Corporation Finance is in charge of setting standards for auditing, financial reporting, and disclosure. This is the division that must review registration statements submitted by corporations issuing new securities, as well as proxy material, annual reports, and any documents that must be filed in connection with mergers or acquisitions.

The Division of Market Regulation oversees the national securities exchanges; registers and regulates securities brokers and dealers; and monitors the self-regulatory organizations of the investment industry, such as the National Association of Securities Dealers (NASD), the organization of over-the-counter (OTC) securities traders. Market Regulation makes sure that securities firms are secure enough financially to protect investors and ensures that sales practices are honest and open.

The Division of Investment Management makes sure that the practices of mutual fund companies and investment advisers are in compliance with the provisions of the Investment Company and Investment Advisers acts of 1940.

The Division of Enforcement investigates possible violations of the securities laws, enforces those laws, and recommends appropriate remedies for consideration by the commission.

The divisions of the SEC work in a variety of ways to carry out their responsibilities.

The NASD offers OTC brokers various computerized services, such as this system, which automatically executes trade orders of 500 or fewer shares.

1. Interpretation and Guidance. Staff members advise companies that are registering securities for sale to the public as well as those considering such a move. Corporate representatives need to know, for example, which documents must be filed when a particular type of security is issued, or what information must be disclosed in a registration statement.

2. Rule making. The securities laws are carried out through SEC rules designed to achieve effective disclosure and regulation with a minimum of burden and expense for all involved. The commission constantly reviews the ways its rules work in practice and makes

changes when needed. In 1983, for example, the SEC adopted Rule 415 permitting *shelf registration* of stocks and bonds. This allows companies that have already issued stock to the public worth at least $150 million to issue additional stock without going through the complete SEC registration process. This rule has increased the speed and reduced the cost to large corporations of issuing new securities.

3. Investigations. If there are inquiries or complaints by investors, or reason to suspect that a violation of the securities laws has occurred, the commission staff must conduct an investigation. Some investigations are triggered by the surprise inspections—conducted by SEC regional offices and the Division of Market Regulation—of the books and records of regulated individuals (such as brokers) and organizations. An investigation may also be called for if the market price of a particular stock changes dramatically, especially if the changes seem unrelated to general market trends or developments in the issuing company or its industry. The SEC may investigate the suspected selling of unregistered securities, or misrepresentation or omission of financial or other important information in a company's registration statement.

4. Imposing Sanctions. If an investigation uncovers violations, the commission may apply to the appropriate federal court for a civil injunction to prohibit the alleged illegal acts or practices. Or the commission may hold its own administrative hearings, which are similar to trials in a court of law. If a hearing finds that a securities firm has violated a law, the commission may suspend or expel the firm from the stock exchanges or the NASD. It may also deny, suspend, or revoke brokers' and dealers' registrations, which means they cannot buy or sell securities for customers while the suspension is in effect.

The SEC may also bar individuals temporarily or permanently from employment with a firm that is registered with an exchange or the NASD.

The Offices

The Office of the General Counsel, the chief legal office of the SEC, handles all court cases in which the commission is involved.

The Office of the Chief Accountant initiates and revises accounting and auditing standards and drafts rules and regulations concerning requirements for the financial statements that are included in disclosure reports.

The Directorate of Economic and Policy Analysis and the Office of the Chief Economist both analyze the effects of SEC rules and regulations on the workings of the securities markets. These offices use masses of financial information, stored in computer files or data bases, to create computer models that simulate the way the economy works. With these models they try to predict, for example, the impact of a particular rule change on the market. The purpose of this research is to determine whether new commission action is necessary to protect investors.

The Office of Administrative Law Judges conducts hearings if investigations suggest possible violations. The SEC judges have only civil authority. If a case involves fraud or other willful violation of the law, the commission may refer it to the Justice Department with a recommendation for criminal prosecution of the offenders.

The Office of Consumer Affairs and Information Services reviews public complaints against entities regulated by the commission. Many matters requiring investigation are first brought to the commission's attention through this office. This is also where investors can get information that publicly held corporations and the secu-

A broker uses a NASD computer system to solve a trading problem.

rities industry are supposed to make available to interested consumers. In every commission office around the country, interested investors may read the registration statements, prospectuses, and annual and quarterly reports of securities firms and companies that sell stock to the public.

Self-regulatory Organizations

The Securities Exchange Act of 1934 not only required the national securities exchanges to register with the SEC, it also gave them the responsibility of creating their own affiliated self-regulatory organizations (SROs) to monitor the activities of their member firms. The SROs carry out many of the regulations of the SEC and in addition impose regulations of their own that may be even more stringent than the commission's. The three major SROs are the New York Stock Exchange, the American Stock Exchange (AMEX), and the NASD.

The SROs monitor many aspects of the operation and sales practices of their member firms in order to prevent and detect violations of securities regulations. They also examine the qualifications of applicants for the position of registered representative (a stockbroker or account executive who executes trades for investors). Applicants must pass both an investigation into their business background and credentials, and an examination of their knowledge of the securities industry (the Series Seven exam, which is administered by the NASD).

The SROs also prescreen upon request publicity and advertising material put out by their member firms, and spot check various publications of those firms, such as market letters and research reports, to ensure that fair and honest information is given out to the public.

One way the SROs watch the activities of member firms is by examining reports of their operational and financial conditions. Depending on the size of the firm, these reports must be submitted either monthly or quarterly. However, if there is a problem with a specific firm or the stock market as a whole, an SRO may require weekly or even daily reports.

Another way in which regulations are enforced is by computer monitoring of trading in stocks. When a security is entered into the NASDAQ system, price and volume limits are also entered, based on the price and volume. patterns for comparable stocks. As the prices at which investors are willing to buy or sell the stock are fed into the system, a computer compares them to the programmed limits. When a new quotation reaches or exceeds the limits, the computer system alerts the NASDAQ's Market Surveillance Section. Then, a professional analyst studies all available data to determine whether there is a logical business-related reason for the unusual activity. Research on such a problem would include questioning the market makers who handle trades in that company's stock, as well as reviewing the 40 categories of reports generated periodically by NASDAQ computers. If there have been no unusual developments in the company, its industry, or the overall economy that might explain the unusual activity, then the NASD begins an investigation into what may be a case of insider trading or market manipulation.

If the investigation shows that violations have occurred, the NASD, like the other SROs, can discipline member firms by imposing fines or ordering temporary or permanent suspensions.

Another activity of SROs is to advise listed companies regarding compliance with the securities laws. In the late 1980s several Wall Street brokers were tried and convicted of trading on inside information, which was prohibited under the 1934 act but had never been legally defined. In the absence of a legal definition, the AMEX formulated its own broad definition of *insider*, to assist its member firms and listed companies: All persons who come into possession of material inside information before its public release are considered insiders for purposes of the AMEX's disclosure policies. Such persons include major stockholders, directors, officers, and employees, and frequently also include outside attorneys, accountants, investment bankers, public relations advisers, advertising agencies, consultants, and other independent contractors. The spouses and other members of the insider's immediate family may also be regarded as insiders. Finally, for purposes of the AMEX's disclosure policy, the term *insiders* also includes "tippees," people who may learn about material inside information.

The company itself is also an insider and, while in possession of material inside information before making it public, is prohibited from buying its own securities from, or selling such securities to, the public in the same manner as other insiders.

Other Laws Affecting Investments

Tax Laws The income from investments is subject to taxation just as the income from other sources is. This income, known as *capital gains*, consists of the difference between the price received when an asset (such as a stock or bond) is sold and the price for which it was bought. For many years the maximum federal tax on capital gains was considerably lower than the tax on earned income. This was a way to encourage investment in the nation's growing industries. There were other tax provisions to cushion capital losses (incurred when a security was sold for less than its original cost) and compensate for the risk of investing. According to the Tax Reform Act of 1986, however, investment income is to be taxed at the same rate as other income. One consequence is that investors' trading decisions can now be based more on investment potential than on tax considerations.

The Securities Investor Protection Act of 1970 This act established the Securities Investor Protection Corporation (SIPC), which protects the customers of registered securities broker-dealers against losses of up to $500,000 if the brokerage fails financially. The SIPC is a government-sponsored, nonprofit corporation funded by its member securities brokerages. All member firms of the national securities exchanges are required by the 1970 law to be members of the SIPC.

State Laws Before the federal securities laws were passed in the 1930s, most states had their own securities laws, which they have maintained over the years. These laws are called "blue sky" laws because they were designed to protect investors from securities issues with "as much investment value as the blue sky." Most state laws require full disclosure on the part of the issuer and stipulate that securities must be registered before they can be sold in the state. Most states now allow coordinated registration so that when SEC registration becomes effective, state registration takes effect also.

The Glass-Steagall Act of 1933 In response to the abuses that led to the stock market crash of 1929 and the banking panic that followed, Congress passed the Glass-Steagall Act in 1933. It prevented commercial banks (full-service banks that make loans and offer both savings and checking services) from underwriting corporate securities and selling securities to the public. Other provisions of Glass-Steagall created the Federal Deposit Insurance Corporation (FDIC) to guarantee individuals' deposits in member banks and gave additional regulatory power to the Federal Reserve Board. These provisions were designed to restore

Secretary of the Treasury William H. Woodin watches President Franklin D. Roosevelt sign the Glass-Steagall Act of 1933, which regulated banking practices.

depositors' confidence in the nation's banks by protecting their money and to safeguard the banking system from fluctuations in the securities markets.

TRENDS IN INVESTMENTS AND THE LAW

Until 1975 the New York Stock Exchange specified the minimum commission to be paid to member brokers by investors when buying or selling securities. Such fixed commissions meant that a customer who traded a few thousand dollars worth of stock at a time was charged the same percentage as a customer trading many times as much. An SEC ruling provided that, as of May 1, 1975, commission rates were to be negotiated between investors and brokers. This meant that large buyers—such as bank trust departments, union pension funds, and large corporations—could bargain with a brokerage and pay lower commission rates than less active investors. Brokers could now try to attract investors' accounts by offering lower rates than their competitors do.

This commission-rate ruling marked the start of a trend toward deregulation in the investment industry. Over the next 12 years, discount brokerages developed, charging lower commission rates, and providing fewer services such as research and advice, to customers. Commercial banks set up discount brokerages as subsidiaries. This put a crack in the Glass-Steagall wall that had kept commercial bankers out of the securities business.

In the late 1980s, commercial banks urged the demolition of the rest of the wall between commercial and investment banking. They pressed Congress to repeal or amend Glass-Steagall so that they could enter the lucrative business of underwriting stock issues for corporations as

A courtroom sketch of five Wall Street brokers indicted in 1986 on charges of insider trading. Their lawyer (second from right) represents them before the presiding federal judge.

well as selling securities directly to the public. By late 1987, several economic policy makers were in agreement that banks should be able to compete in some areas with brokerages, as long as their investment divisions would be subject to SEC regulation.

At the same time, the insider trading scandals that erupted on Wall Street in 1986 led to demands for tighter regulation. If legislation is enacted, the most likely moves will be to define *insider trading*, and to toughen the penalties for individuals and firms found to be in violation of the law.

REGULATION AND WORK ON WALL STREET

Every working day of their lives, account executives and investment bankers must deal with the laws, rules, and regulations we have been discussing. Indeed, they must become familiar with them in order to pass an examination and register with an exchange as brokers and underwriters.

Brokers and Trading Restrictions   Regulations permeate the daily life of account executives. When they make recommendations to clients, they must obey the "suitability" or "know-thy-customer" rule that is common to all major exchanges. The suitability of a particular security for a particular investor is determined partly by the investment goals a customer specifies when opening an account at a brokerage. A statement of the investor's goals is entered on a new-account form; if an investor later brings a complaint, the account executive can refer to the form as part of a defense. A new-account form also must contain information about the customer's overall financial situation. The broker must consider this when recommending certain types of speculative investments. As an account executive learns a customer's investment history and level of sophistication, these factors too should enter into the suitability decision. Also according to the suitability rule, for riskier forms of investing, especially margin accounts or options trading, an account executive must be extremely careful that the investor can afford the losses that might be incurred.

Firms police their AE's for churning—the rapid buying and selling of stocks for the sole purpose of generating commissions. Churning is most likely to occur when an investor has opened a discretionary account, which authorizes the AE to execute transactions without consulting the investor. An account executive who exceeds the normal range of trades for a client must fill out a questionnaire to explain the activity to the brokerage firm management. As part of its periodic examination of member firms, the Exchange also examines accounts for churning and has a rule that commissions cannot exceed a certain percentage of the value of an account.

NASD regulations also prohibit account executives from trading in *hot stocks*—new issues that might be particularly desirable immediately after an initial offering—for their own accounts or for the accounts of their firms or certain other members of the securities industry. The reason for this rule is to make sure that investment professionals and firms do not trade for their own advantage at the expense of the public.

Documentation   An account executive must make sure that new customers sign a customer agreement, which specifies the rights and obligations of the customer and the broker, and states that all disputes are to be settled by arbitration. The AE also must complete a new-account form for each customer. Account executives must complete an order ticket whenever a client instructs them to buy or sell securities, even though such orders are usually given over the phone. After a transaction takes place, the brokerage must send a confirmation letter to the client. This letter, along with the monthly statement of account activity, allows the client to verify that the account executive has conducted the transactions as requested.

Regulation and Investment Bankers   The workday of investment bankers is affected by both the requirement for disclosure and the prohibitions against fraud and manipulation in the securities markets. With regard to disclosure, investment bankers must observe *due diligence* when they underwrite a public issue of a company's securities. This means that they must make a reasonable effort to determine that the information in the registration statement is accurate and complete. This usually involves on-site inspection of the company's facilities and meetings with its key managers. If investment bankers do not perform this duty well and mistakes or omissions appear, they or their firms are financially liable to investors who may lose money as a result of their lack of diligence.

Investment bankers are also required to make sure that no shares of a new issue are traded before the sale of a stock or a merger or acquisition is announced publicly.

PROTECTING YOURSELF IN THE SECURITIES MARKETS

According to *What Every Investor Should Know*, published by the Securities and Exchange Commission, investors can protect themselves by observing these 10 basic safeguards:

1. Don't buy securities offered by telephone or through "cold calls" from an unknown broker. Before buying securities, get all the relevant information in writing.
2. Beware of account executives who try to pressure you into acting immediately.
3. Don't buy on tips or rumors. Not only is it safer to get the facts first, it is illegal to buy or sell securities based on inside information that is not generally available to other investors.
4. Get professional advice if you don't understand something in a prospectus or a piece of sales literature.
5. Be skeptical of promises of quick profits.
6. Check on the credentials of anyone you don't know who tries to sell you securities.
7. Remember that prior success is no guarantee of future success in an investment arrangement.
8. Be especially careful with any investments intended as tax shelters. (The Tax Reform Act of 1986 has decreased the opportunities to shelter income from taxation.)
9. Be sure you understand the risk of loss in trading securities.
10. Don't speculate. Speculation can be a useful investment tool for those who can understand and manage the risks involved. But for the average investor, speculating is more akin to gambling than investing.

PROTECTION FOR INVESTORS: HOW TO COMPLAIN

Investors who believe that a broker has dealt with them unfairly have the right to complain. According to the NASD, the most common customer complaints against member firms involve slow delivery of securities certificates and delayed transfer of customer accounts from one brokerage to another. Most of these problems are easily resolved.

More serious are charges that an account was churned or that an account executive has consistently recommended the purchase of securities incompatible with a customer's investment goals. In such a case, the answers entered on a new-account form when the client began working with the AE, specifying a certain investment goal, would be compared with the broker's recommendations.

An investor who is thinking of complaining about a firm or an account executive should keep all records of transactions and statements from the brokerage and make careful notes of all telephone conversations. The investor should first express dissatisfaction either to the AE or to his or her supervisor. If that does not solve the problem, the investor should report the problem to the SRO—an exchange or the NASD—to which the offending firm belongs. Investors may also report questionable securities practices to the SEC's Office of Consumer Affairs. An investor who is still not satisfied may begin arbitration proceedings against the account executive or, if it is a question of supervision, against the brokerage firm.

Arbitration resembles a courtroom trial in that a hearing of the issues and positions of both sides takes place, and a decision is reached. However, arbitration proceedings occur outside the judicial system and do not involve a jury. Securities arbitration cases are managed by the responsible SRO and decided by majority vote of a panel whose three members, appointed by the SRO, serve as judges. One panel member represents the securities industry and is likely to be either a retired member of that group or someone affiliated with a firm other than one involved in the case being heard. The other panel judges are called "public" members and have no relationship to the industry. They are often lawyers.

The securities industry prefers arbitration because cases are usually settled at less expense and more quickly that way. In arbitration, cases can be argued by staff lawyers, whereas court cases require more expensive outside counsel.

Arbitration can result in disciplinary action against an account executive or a firm, such as a fine or temporary suspension from the SRO. It can also result in the payment of damages to the investor.

Most investors, when opening a brokerage account, sign an agreement to abide by the results of arbitration. Despite the agreement, most investors, believing that they would fare better in a jury trial, have preferred over the years to rely on the courts. Before 1987, some lower courts had held that arbitration agreements were not always enforceable. However, if both parties agreed to arbitration, the arbitration board's decision was enforceable. In 1987 the Supreme Court ruled that brokerage firms may insist that customers abide by the agreement to arbitrate all charges brought under the Securities Exchange Act of 1934.

The issue of how disputes are to be settled is an important one for the securities industry. Between 1980 and 1986 the number of arbitration cases handled by the Exchange tripled, from 327 to 1,004, and the number of NASD arbitration claims grew fivefold, from 300 to 1,500. One reason for the growth of arbitration cases is the great increase in the volume of trading. Another is that investors are becoming more sophisticated and aware of their rights. Many observers believe that still another reason lies in the less regulated, more competitive atmosphere that has prevailed on Wall Street since 1975, which may offer more opportunities for fraud and manipulation.

CAREERS IN INVESTMENTS AND THE LAW

There are many positions open to lawyers, qualified paralegal personnel, and other professionals, in the investment industry and the related government agencies.

Staffing the SEC   The Securities and Exchange Commission has a staff of about 2,100, of whom 1,350 are based in Washington, D.C., with the other 750 situated in 14 offices around the country. More than 700 staff members are lawyers, many of whom work in the Enforcement and Market Regulation divisions. There are also many accountants employed by the SEC, some of whom are certified public accountants (CPAs, accountants who have passed a formal examination). The SEC also hires economists—people trained in financial analysis—both with or without a master of business administration (MBA) degree.

Staffing the NASD   The National Association of Securities Dealers, like the SEC, is headquartered in Washington, D.C., where most of its 1,700 employees work. There are also 14 district offices, the largest being in New York, Chicago, and Los Angeles. The NASD hires attorneys who know securities law and people with finance and accounting backgrounds to serve as examiners. It also has other positions suited to people who are comfortable working with numbers and details, as well as those who can deal tactfully with the association's 6,700 member firms. The NASD runs a large, sophisticated computer network and also hires many people to work in systems planning, design, and operations.

Staffing the Exchange and the AMEX   The New York Stock Exchange and the American Stock Exchange each

Jeannie Davitt, a legal secretary with Stroock & Stroock & Lavan, a Wall Street law firm that represents investment banking firms.

employ about 200 people—all in New York City—to enforce SEC and internal regulations. People who work in the compliance divisions of these exchanges are the detectives who look for questionable trading patterns. They must have experience working in the operations area of a securities firm as well as training in finance, mathematics, or business. Lawyers in the exchanges' legal and regulatory divisions hold hearings when a violation of rules is charged.

The New York Stock Exchange has examiners with legal and accounting backgrounds who regularly audit the records of member firms to make sure their own financial condition and their interactions with customers conform to Exchange rules.

Litigation associate Nelson Boxer uses LEXIS, a computerized legal research system, in the library of Stroock & Stroock & Lavan.

Legal Work in Securities Firms   Securities firms employ lawyers and other professionals. The positions are varied. For example, lawyers, finance experts, and accounting specialists staff the compliance departments, whose tasks include computer analysis of trading patterns for evidence of possible stock manipulation or fraud. These firms' lawyers also check to make sure that account executives—and securities—are registered in the states where clients live. Finally, it is the legal department's responsibility to furnish information about account executives and trading patterns in response to queries from an SRO.

Private Law Firms in the Investment Industry   General securities legal work representing investment firms, most of which is carried out in New York City, involves working with both investment bankers and companies selling stock to the public, to make sure that the SEC disclosure rules are observed. Lawyers might be employed in this work immediately after graduation from law school or after having worked for the SEC or an SRO for a few years. Firms with a Wall Street practice also advise brokerages and investment bankers with regard to laws and regulations applicable to the industry itself. These law firms also provide trial lawyers when necessary to represent client securities firms in court.

Legal Departments of Corporations   The staff or in-house lawyers for publicly held corporations work with outside lawyers and investment bankers on underwritings of the companies' securities issues. They are responsible, along with the companies' finance departments and auditors, for the financial reports that must be filed periodically with the SEC. They monitor officers and directors to ensure that they file the required documents when they trade in the company's stock. They are also responsible for responding to inquiries from the SEC or an SRO.

Public Accounting Firms   Public accounting firms hire accountants, most of whom must be certified public accountants. Accounting firms must audit the financial statements required by the SEC and the SROs in order to certify that these records accurately present a company's financial position in accordance with generally accepted auditing standards.

FURTHER READING

American Stock Exchange. *American Stock Exchange Disclosure Policies*. New York: American Stock Exchange, 1983. Question-and-answer format explains how the AMEX complies with the SEC's disclosure requirements.

Bining, Arthur Cecil, and Thomas C. Cochran. *The Rise of American Economic Life*. New York: Scribner, 1964. A comprehensive, well-written economic history.

Calhoun, Mary E. *How to Get the Hot Jobs in Business and Finance*. New York: Harper/Perennial Library, 1986. Detailed information about various workplaces in the financial world.

Epstein, Rachel S., and Nina Liebman. *Biz Speak: A Dictionary of Business Terms, Slang, and Jargon*. New York: Franklin Watts, 1986. The language of the investment world, from boardrooms to back rooms.

Ingrassa, Lawrence. "For SEC, Developing Insider-Trading Cases Is Frustrating Work." *Wall Street Journal*, July 2, 1986. Fascinating look at how the SEC attempts to trace insider trading.

NASDAQ Handbook: The Stockmarket of Tomorrow—Today. Chicago: Probus, 1977. How the over-the-counter market operates and is regulated.

New York Stock Exchange. *Just and Equitable Principles of Trade: A Summary of Regulation and Surveillance*. New York: New York Stock Exchange, 1982. How the Exchange regulates its member firms.

New York Stock Exchange. *Understanding Stocks* and *Understanding Bonds*. New York: New York Stock Exchange, 1988. Short, basic descriptions.

U.S. Securities and Exchange Commission. *What Every Investor Should Know*. Washington: Government Printing Office, 1986. Pamphlet primer about how to be a good investment consumer.

U.S. Securities and Exchange Commission. *The Work of the SEC*. Washington: Government Printing Office, 1986. The Securities laws and how they are carried out by the SEC.

GLOSSARY

account executive (AE), stockbroker, broker An agent who acts as an intermediary between buyers and sellers of securities.

acquisition Any process in which one company gains control over another.

audit The professional examination of a corporation's or individual's financial statement.

bankruptcy The inability of a corporation or individual to meet financial obligations; also, legal status that protects the corporation or individual from losing personal property to creditors.

"blue-sky" laws State laws that protect investors by prohibiting the misrepresentation of securities. These laws require that specific information be given to prospective investors.

bond A certificate that represents a loan to a company or government agency. The issuing company (the borrower) pays interest for the use of the money and must repay the entire amount (principal) of the bond at a specified time.

brokerage, brokerage firm, or **investment firm** An organization that facilitates the buying and selling of stocks and other types of investments. Account executives are employed by investment firms.

churning A stockbroker's illegal practice of buying and selling clients' securities frequently for the purpose of generating commissions.

due diligence The investigation (especially by underwriters) of a company proposing to make a public offering, to verify the accuracy of its prospectus.

earnings A company's revenues minus its costs, expenses, and taxes; figured before paying dividends.

Federal Deposit Insurance Corporation (FDIC) The U.S. government agency that guarantees depositors in member banks against loss.

Federal Reserve System The central banking system of the United States, which supervises the nation's banking system and sets appropriate monetary policy.

insider trading Illegal stock transactions that take advantage of confidential information to make a personal profit.

margin account A brokerage account in which the client deposits a minimum amount to purchase securities, borrowing the remainder from the broker. In exchange for margin credit, the client pays interest to the broker.

merger Any process by which two or more separate companies combine to form a single company.

monopoly A corporation that has little or no competition in its industry and can therefore control prices in the marketplace.

mutual fund An investment in which the money of many shareholders is combined in order to invest in a wide range of securities.

NASDAQ (pronounced "nazdak") The computerized National Association of Securities Dealers Automatic Quotations system, which provides price quotations on stocks and bonds traded over the counter. The National Association of Securities Dealers (NASD) is the organization of broker/dealers who handle the securities traded over the counter.

prospectus A publication issued by an investment company or corporation to meet SEC regulations that describes financial details to prospective investors.

proxy statement Information about votes to be taken at a shareholders' meeting, sent with the notice of the meeting. Votes would be necessary to elect directors and approve a merger or acquisition of the company. The accompanying proxy card, when filled out, signed, and mailed, constitutes formal authorization for someone to vote on behalf of the shareholder at the meeting.

Securities and Exchange Commission (SEC) A U.S. government agency established by Congress in 1934 to regulate the trading of stocks and bonds to protect investors.

self-regulatory organization (SRO) The securities exchanges, such as the New York Stock Exchange, the American Stock Exchange, and the National Association of Securities Dealers, that regulate and monitor the activities of member firms.

share of stock Any of the equal parts into which the entire value, or equity, of a company is divided. It represents part ownership in the company.

shelf registration Registration process for offering stocks and bonds to the public; available to companies with at least $150 million in stock held by outside investors; expedites the registration process required for an initial public offering.

takeover The acquisition of one company by another.

tender offer Process by which an acquiring company or investor attempts to gain control over an unwilling target company by buying as much of the outstanding stock of the target company as possible; stockholders are asked to tender their shares to the acquiring party. Also called a "hostile takeover."

trust The consolidation of companies in the same industry for the purpose of reducing competition and fixing prices.

underwriting The process of buying newly issued securities from a corporation and reselling them to the public. Investment banking firms underwrite new issues.

INDEX

RACHEL S. EPSTEIN, a free-lance writer specializing in business subjects, holds an M.B.A. from New York University. Her articles have appeared in the *Wall Street Journal*, the *Washington Post*, *Working Woman*, and *Ms*. She is the coauthor also of *Biz Speak: A Dictionary of Business Terms, Slang and Jargon*.

PAUL A. SAMUELSON, senior editorial consultant, is Institute Professor Emeritus at the Massachusetts Institute of Technology. He is author (now coauthor) of the best-selling textbook *Economics*. He served as an adviser to President John F. Kennedy and in 1970 was the first American to win the Nobel Prize in economics.

SHAWN PATRICK BURKE, consulting editor, is a securities analyst with Standard & Poor's Corporation. He has been an internal consultant in industry as well as for a Wall Street investment firm, and he has extensive experience in computer-generated financial modeling and analysis.